IGNEOUS ROCKS

BY M. J. YORK

Published by The Child's World®
1980 Lookout Drive • Mankato, MN 56003-1705
800-599-READ • www.childsworld.com

Acknowledgments
The Child's World®: Mary Swensen, Publishing Director
Red Line Editorial: Editorial direction and production
The Design Lab: Design

Design Element: Shutterstock Images
Photographs ©: Shutterstock Images, cover (top), cover
(bottom left), 1 (top), 1 (bottom left); Eduard Andras/
iStockphoto, cover (bottom right), 1 (bottom right), 11, 15,
18; iStockphoto, 5, 7, 8, 16, 17, 20; John Anderson Photo/
iStockphoto, 6; Israel Hervas Bengochea/Shutterstock
Images, 9; Tarek El Sombati/iStockphoto, 13, 23; Justin
Reznick/iStockphoto, 19

ISBN 9781503808010
LCCN 2015958139

Printed in the United States of America
Mankato, MN
June, 2016
PA02305

ABOUT THE AUTHOR

M. J. York is a children's author and editor. She likes to travel and identify the rocks she sees in different parts of the country. York lives in Minnesota.

CONTENTS

CHAPTER 1

What Are Igneous Rocks?

The earth shakes, and birds take flight. Suddenly, burning rocks and ash shoot high into the sky. Fiery lava rolls slowly down the mountainside. A volcano is erupting.

A volcano is a mountain or hill with a vent at the top. A volcanic eruption happens when gas and melted rock burst out of the vent. **Reservoirs** of melted rock are deep underground. An eruption brings the melted rock to the surface.

When it is underground, the melted rock is called magma. Melted rock that reaches the surface is called lava. When magma or lava cools, it forms **igneous rocks**. There are many types of igneous rocks. They can have many colors and textures. You can find igneous rocks in many places around the world.

Geologists are scientists who study rocks. They divide igneous rocks into two categories. Some rocks form deep below Earth's surface. These are called **intrusive** rocks.

During a volcanic eruption, lava bursts out of a volcano vent.

Other rocks form above or near the surface. These are called **extrusive** rocks.

Intrusive rocks form slowly. Most magma stays deep under the ground. It takes thousands or even millions of years to cool. Intrusive rocks have a rough texture.

Granite is one type of intrusive rock.

Extrusive rocks form quickly. When lava leaves a volcano, it begins cooling right away. The lava surface hardens first. Rock under the surface becomes solid over weeks or months. Some volcanoes are underwater. They erupt into oceans. Lava that erupts into water cools even more quickly. Extrusive rocks have a smooth or fine texture. The faster they cool, the smoother they are.

Igneous rocks can change over time. Natural forces cause them to weather and erode. Wind and water eat away at the rocks. The rocks break into smaller pieces. Eventually, these pieces form into other rocks. This process is called the rock cycle.

THE ROCK CYCLE

Rocks on Earth are slowly but constantly changing. First, melted lava cools into igneous rocks. Heat and pressure transform some of these rocks into metamorphic rocks. Others break down over time. Sedimentary rocks are made of the broken-down pieces of other rocks. Eventually, the rocks are pushed deep under Earth's surface. They melt and the cycle begins again.

Obsidian is one type of extrusive rock.

CHAPTER 2

Layers of Earth

Igneous rocks help scientists learn about Earth's structure. Many are formed by magma from deep under the surface.

Earth has four layers. The top layer is the crust. This thin layer is only 3 to 30 miles (4.8 to 48 km) thick. It is made of solid rocks. Deeper within Earth's surface is the mantle. The mantle is hotter than the crust. Pressure on the mantle is greater. Rocks in the mantle are mostly solid. This layer is approximately 2,000 miles (3,200 km) thick.

The core is the center of Earth. There are two layers: the outer core and the inner core. Each layer is

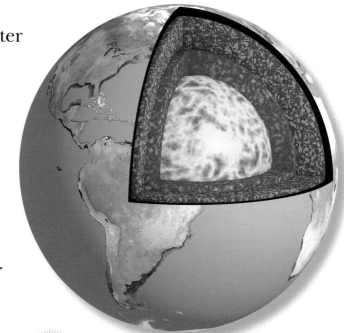

Earth's layers, from outermost to innermost, are the crust, mantle, outer core, and inner core.

extremely hot. It is made of two metals, nickel and iron. The outer core is made of liquid nickel and iron. The inner core is made of solid metals. In the inner core, elements are under extreme heat and pressure. The **atoms** in the metals cannot spread out enough to become liquid. They are packed together in a solid.

Magma forms in the crust and upper mantle. It needs special conditions to form. Heat, pressure, and water can all produce magma. Earth's surface is made of many pieces called tectonic plates. The plates float on top of the lower mantle. Slowly, they move and slide against

Thingvellir National Park in Iceland contains rifts in the surface near the boundaries of tectonic plates.

each other. The movement of the plates makes mountains rise. It also creates earthquakes and volcanoes.

Faults in Earth's surface often occur at boundaries between plates. The plates can interact in three ways. Sometimes, they pull away from each other. They create what is called a divergent boundary. Magma comes up close to the surface in the space between the plates. The magma makes new crust.

Sometimes, one plate gets pushed under another, creating a convergent boundary. The motion of the plates can cause earthquakes. Deep underground, the plate's rocks change form. If they melt, they become magma. Volcanoes rise where the underground magma comes to the surface. When the magma cools, it forms new igneous rocks. Plates pushing together can also form mountains.

Additionally, plates can slide past each other. They create transform boundaries. **Friction** makes the plates catch or lock against each other. Then the plates can suddenly slip free, causing an earthquake. The San Andreas Fault in California is a transform boundary.

Most active volcanoes are located at faults. Volcanoes are also located in places called hot spots. In these places, heat from the lower mantle rises to the surface. Hot spots

TECTONIC PLATE BOUNDARIES

There are three types of tectonic plate boundaries. At a divergent boundary, two plates pull away from each other. At a transform boundary, two plates slide past each other. At a convergent boundary, one plate is pushed under another.

Divergent plate boundary

Transform plate boundary

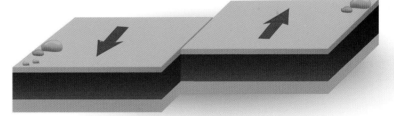

Convergent plate boundary

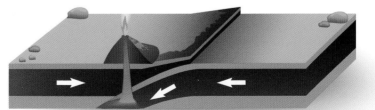

form at plate boundaries. But when the plates move, the hot spots stay in place. Eventually, the volcanoes go extinct. Extinct volcanoes no longer erupt. One hot spot is located under the Hawaiian Islands.

Igneous rocks form at plate boundaries and near volcanoes. Different types of rocks form at the different types of boundaries. Most divergent boundaries are under the ocean. Magma near these boundaries cools quickly. It forms rocks such as basalt.

Basalt is an extrusive igneous rock. It is dark and smooth. Basalt is one of the most common rocks on Earth's surface. Most of it is found in or near oceans. People use crushed basalt in roads and construction projects.

Magma at convergent boundaries can form other types of rock. One type is diorite. Diorite is an intrusive igneous rock. It usually has black and white speckles.

People crush diorite into gravel. They carve it into statues. They use diorite in stone buildings.

Granite also forms at convergent boundaries. It is an intrusive igneous rock. It is light-colored with many speckles. Granite is common on Earth's surface. It is very strong. People can polish granite and make it very smooth. Many buildings are made of granite. People make floors and countertops from granite, too. Mount Rushmore in South Dakota is made from granite. So are the mountains of Yosemite, California.

Basalt is a dark, smooth rock that can form near divergent plate boundaries.

CHAPTER 3

Inside Igneous Rocks

All rocks are made of minerals. Each type of mineral contains different elements. Atoms of these elements combine into compounds. The compounds form a structure called a crystal. Igneous rocks are made of combinations of eight different minerals.

In magma, minerals in rocks melt. The compounds of atoms come apart. The magma is made of elements such as iron, silicon, and sodium. When the magma cools, these elements form new compounds. They become minerals again. This process is called crystallization. Eventually, the minerals form rocks.

Minerals take time to grow. Igneous rocks that cooled slowly contain large crystals. Rocks that cooled quickly contain smaller crystals.

Intrusive igneous rocks form slowly underground. They have large crystals. You can see the different minerals when you look at them. Each color in these rocks is from a different mineral. Granite is an example

CRYSTAL STRUCTURES IN QUARTZ

Quartz is a common mineral in igneous rocks. It is made of silicon and oxygen atoms. The silicon and oxygen bond together in a crystal structure.

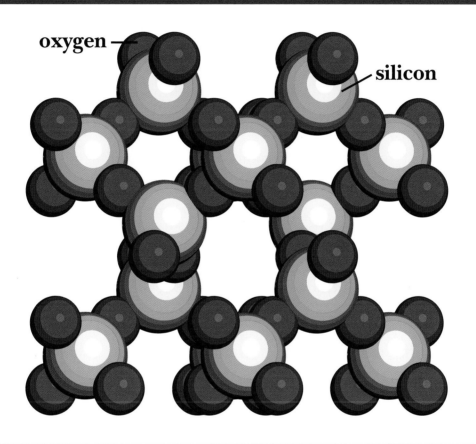

oxygen

silicon

of this kind of rock. Peridotites are another example. Peridotites are a family of rocks. There are many types of peridotites. They are dark-colored. Sometimes, diamonds and other sparkly **gems** are found inside peridotites.

The colors in granite are from its minerals. Most granite is made of the minerals quartz, feldspar, and mica.

These gems form deep in the mantle. The peridotite protects them as they travel to the surface.

Extrusive igneous rocks form quickly near the surface of Earth. They have small crystals. The crystals had little time to grow. Geologists might use a microscope to see them. Rhyolite is an example of extrusive rock. This rock is often pinkish. It contains very small crystals. Sometimes, gems are found inside. Rhyolite forms so quickly that air pockets are sometimes left inside. Later, new minerals fill the air pockets. Gems such as topaz, agates, and opals can form.

Sometimes lava cools so quickly that crystals cannot form. Obsidian is a type of igneous rock that forms quickly. Sometimes it forms when hot lava hits water. It has few or no crystals. Obsidian is very smooth. It is often dark. When obsidian breaks, it has sharp edges. In ancient times, people made knives and cutting tools from obsidian.

When they find igneous rocks, geologists look for crystals. The crystals can help them identify the type of rock.

PERIDOTITES AND A CHANGING CLIMATE

Peridotites have a special property. Their minerals bind to carbon dioxide. This means the rocks can capture or soak up carbon dioxide. Researchers are studying this process. Too much carbon dioxide can cause the climate to change. People might be able to use peridotites to take carbon dioxide out of the air. This process could help slow climate change.

Topaz, a gem, can form inside rhyolite or granite.

CHAPTER 4

Igneous Rocks around Us

Igneous rocks are all around us. They come in many different shapes and sizes. Different factors affect the shapes of the rocks. One is how quickly the rocks cool. Natural forces, such as wind and water, are also factors. These forces wear away rock. They change rocks' shape over time.

Some igneous rocks are **porous**. They have many tiny holes. Pumice is one example. It is an extrusive rock. When pumice is formed, lava cools so quickly that gases cannot escape. Air bubbles from the gases form tiny holes. The holes allow pumice to float in water. People use pumice in concrete. It makes the concrete lightweight.

Porous igneous rocks contain many holes.

Larger gas pockets can leave behind stone bubbles. Sometimes, these are lined with minerals or crystals. Other minerals fill the cracks or holes.

Water affects rocks' shapes, too. Some igneous rocks form underwater. They have different shapes than the igneous rocks that form on land. Basalt sometimes forms underwater. It can form in pillow shapes. Lava flows slowly, but it cools quickly. It bulges under a crust of hardened magma. Rounded shapes form as the basalt hardens. If the crust breaks, the escaping lava forms another pillow.

Lava flows slowly across the surface of Earth.

Deep underground, large pockets of magma cool. Igneous rocks form large structures. These are called **intrusions**. Some form along faults or cracks. Others form near volcanoes. We can see some on Earth's surface. Softer rocks above the intrusions erode away. Eventually, the igneous rocks are exposed. This process can take millions of years. Devil's Tower in Wyoming is one intrusion that has been exposed.

Devil's Tower is one example of a rock intrusion.

Volcanoes are made of igneous rocks, too. Different magma conditions cause different types of volcanoes to form. Cinder cone volcanoes have one vent in the center. Lava erupts out from the vent. As it cools, the volcano grows taller. Cinder cone volcanoes can grow quickly.

Stratovolcanoes are made of lava, ash, and rock. They are taller than cinder cone volcanoes. They build up in layers through many eruptions. These volcanoes erupt very violently.

In shield volcanoes, lava flows away instead of building up. As a result, the lava becomes thin. Shield volcanoes do not grow very tall. But they can be very wide. When a shield volcano erupts, the lava may harden in a dome shape.

We build beautiful buildings with granite. We crush other igneous rocks into gravel. Some igneous rocks contain gems or valuable minerals. Igneous rocks are all around us. Have you seen any in your neighborhood?

VOLCANOES ON MARS

Volcanoes have erupted on other planets, too. In 2009, robot vehicles analyzed rocks on Mars. They found that basalt is common in Mars rocks. Some of the basalt is from a giant shield volcano, Olympus Mons. It is the largest volcano in the solar system.

atoms *(AT-uhmz)* Atoms are the smallest parts of an element that have all the properties of that element. Atoms bond together to make compounds.

climate *(KLY-mit)* Climate is the usual weather in a particular place. Too much carbon dioxide in the air can change the climate on Earth.

extrusive *(ex-TROO-siv)* Extrusive rocks form from melted rock above or near Earth's surface. Basalt is a type of extrusive igneous rock.

faults *(FAWLTS)* Faults are cracks in Earth's crust, often located at boundaries between tectonic plates. Faults can cause earthquakes.

friction *(FRIK-shun)* Friction occurs when two things rub against each other. The force of friction can affect Earth's tectonic plates.

gems *(JEMZ)* Crystallized minerals that are valued for their beauty are called gems. Some igneous rocks contain gems.

geologists *(jee-OL-uh-jists)* Geologists are scientists who study rocks. Geologists might analyze the layers in a rock to learn how old it is.

igneous rocks *(IG-nee-us ROKS)* Igneous rocks are formed from melted magma or lava. Magma cools and then hardens into igneous rocks.

intrusions *(in-TROO-zhunz)* Intrusions are large underground formations of igneous rocks. Intrusions form when magma solidifies underground.

intrusive *(in-TROO-siv)* Intrusive rocks form from melted rock deep underground. Magma that hardens underground forms intrusive rocks.

porous *(POH-rus)* When something is porous, water or air can enter it. Igneous rocks with holes are porous.

pressure *(PRESH-ur)* Pressure is the force made by pressing on something. Wind and water create pressure that can change the shape and texture of a rock.

reservoirs *(REH-zer-vworz)* Reservoirs are large spaces where liquids collect. Magma collects in reservoirs underground.

IN THE LIBRARY

Brown, Cynthia Light, and Nick Brown. *Explore Rocks and Minerals!*
White River Junction, VT: Nomad Press, 2010.

Tomecek, Steve. *Everything Rocks and Minerals*.
Washington, DC: National Geographic, 2010.

Van Rose, Susanna. *Volcano & Earthquake*. New York: DK Publishing, 2014.

ON THE WEB

Visit our Web site for links about igneous rocks: **childsworld.com/links**

*Note to Parents, Teachers, and Librarians: We routinely verify our Web links to make
sure they are safe and active sites. So encourage your readers to check them out!*

INDEX